Telling Tails

By Allan Fowler

Consultants

Linda Cornwell, Learning Resource Consultant,
Indiana Department of Education

Sharyn Fenwick, Elementary Science/Math Specialist,
Gustavus Adolphus College, St. Peter, Minnesota

Children's Press®
A Division of Grolier Publishing
New York   London   Hong Kong   Sydney
Danbury, Connecticut

Visit Children's Press® on the Internet at:
http://publishing.grolier.com

Designer: Herman Adler Design Group

Library of Congress Cataloging–in–Publication Data

Fowler, Allan.
    Telling Tails / by Allan Fowler.
      p. cm. — (Rookie read-about science)
    Includes index.
    Summary: Describes different kinds of tails and their purposes, examining
both animals and objects such as airplanes and kites.
    ISBN 0-516-20803-9 (lib. bdg.)   0-516-26368-4 (pbk.)
    1. Tail—Juvenile literature. [1. Tail. 2. Animals—Habits and behavior.]
I. Title. II. Series.
QL950.6.F68   1998   97-23299
591.47—dc21   CIP
                                                  AC

A happy dog wags its tail.
What kind of tail? That
depends on the dog.

Some dogs have short tails,
some have long ones.

Some have thick tails,
some have thin ones.

Some dogs' tails point
back, or up, or down . . .
or curl over a dog's back.

Dogs' tails are just a small
part of the tale of the tail.

Most animals have tails. Imagine how many different kinds of tails there are! Pigs' tails are curly.

Squirrels' tails are bushy.

A horse's tail is a bunch
of long hairs. Rabbits have
very short, fluffy tails.

As big as an elephant is,
it has a small, skinny tail.

Apes, such as chimps and gorillas, have no tails at all . . .

Gorilla

but most monkeys have tails.

Dogs wag their tails. But tails are good for other things, too. A horse's tail can brush away flies.

Beavers in rivers warn
each other of danger by
slapping the water with
their flat tails.

Tails can help animals get around. Some monkeys swing on branches with their tails.

Kangaroos use their long, strong tails to keep their balance—and take those big leaps.

Most fish swim by waving their tails from side to side.

American alligator

Crocodiles and alligators
use their tails for swimming.
Also, with one swipe of its
tail, a croc or gator can stun
a small animal, or knock it
into the water.

The strangest tails are found on some kinds of lizards and salamanders.

Their tails break off when they are grabbed by an enemy.

No problem. The lizard soon grows a new one!

19

Male birds often have big sets of tail feathers. This tom turkey spreads his feathers out proudly so a female will notice him.

The female bird's feathers
are not as fancy.

Perhaps the prettiest
tail feathers belong to
male peacocks—green
and blue and gold, with
spots like eyes.

23

Snakes' tails are
a real puzzle.

Where does a snake's body end and its tail begin?

Not all tails are on animals. Things that look like animal tails are sometimes called tails. We talk about the tails of airplanes . . .

# of kites . . .

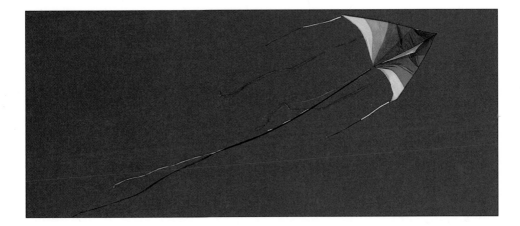

and of comets.

Why do you think one side of a coin is called "heads," and the other side is called "tails?"

Or why is this sentence the "tail end" of this book?

Words You Know

tail

comet

alligator

gorilla

kangaroo

monkey

peacock

rabbit

squirrel

Index

airplanes, 26
alligators, 17, 30
apes, 10
beavers, 13
coins, 28-29
comets, 27, 30
crocodiles, 17
dogs, 3-5, 12
elephants, 9
feathers, 20-21, 22-23
females, 20-21
fish, 16
horses, 8, 12
kangaroos, 15, 31
kites, 27
lizards, 18-19
males, 20, 22
monkeys, 11, 14, 31

peacocks, 22-23, 31
pigs, 6
rabbits, 8, 31
shape, 4-5
size, 4-5
snakes, 24-25
squirrels, 7, 31
turkeys, 20-21
uses
    brushing away flies, 12
    defense, 18
    leaping, 15
    for show, 20
    swimming, 16-17
    swinging, 14
    wagging, 3, 12
    warnings, 13
    as weapons, 17

About the Author

Allan Fowler is a freelance writer with a background in advertising. Born in New York, he now lives in Chicago and enjoys traveling.

Photo Credits

©: Animals Animals: 10, 30 bottom right (Roger Aitkenhead), 12 (Robert Maier); Comstock: 3, 5 bottom left, 21; Jim Merli: 25; Omni-Photo Communications: 11 (B. Richmond Smith); Photo Researchers: 15, 31 top right (Bill Bachman), 24 (S.L. & J.T. Collins), 5 top, 9, 30 top left (Tim Davis), 23, 31 middle right (Gregory G. Dimijian), 8 right, 31 bottom left (Jerry L. Ferrara), 26 (George Haling), 17, 30 bottom left (Tom & Pat Leeson), 27 bottom, 30 top right (Jerry Lodriguss), cover (Renee Lynn), 14, 31 top left (Tom McHugh), 7, 31 bottom right (Gregory K. Scott), 29 (Day Williams); Valan Photos: 19 (Jim Merli); Visuals Unlimited: 6, 13 (John D. Cunningham), 16 (Dave B. Fleetham), 20 (Charlie Heidecker), 27 top (W. Ormerod), 8 left (Barry Slaven), 5 bottom right (John Sohiden).